DRAGON FIELD GUIDES

DRAGON *Behavior*

A Field Guide

TAYLOR FENMORE

Lerner Publications ◆ Minneapolis

Lerner Publications Company
An imprint of Lerner Publishing Group, Inc.
241 First Avenue North
Minneapolis, MN 55401 USA

For reading levels and more information, look up this title at www.lernerbooks.com.

Main body text set in Aptifer Sans LT Pro.
Typeface provided by Linotype AG.

Editor: Angel Kidd **Designer:** Athena Currier **Photo Editor:** Angel Kidd
Lerner team: Martha Kranes

Library of Congress Cataloging-in-Publication Data

Names: Fenmore, Taylor, author.
Title: Dragon behavior : a field guide / Taylor Fenmore.
Description: Minneapolis : Lerner Publications , [2026] | Series: Dragon field guides | Includes bibliographical references and index. | Audience term: Preteens | Audience term: Middle school students | Audience: Ages 8–11 | Audience: Grades 4–6 | Summary: "From breathing fire to bringing rain, dragons around the world are believed to behave in many ways. Readers will discover the life cycle of dragons, how they interact with humans, their motivations, and more"—Provided by publisher.
Identifiers: LCCN 2024039818 | ISBN 9798765669297 (library binding) | ISBN 9798765683965 (paperback) | ISBN 9798765676899 (epub)
Subjects: LCSH: Dragons—Juvenile literature.
Classification: LCC GR830.D7 F47 2026 | DDC 398.24/54—dc23/eng/20240927

LC record available at https://lccn.loc.gov/2024039818

Manufactured in the United States of America
1-1011745-53900-12/12/2024

Table of Contents

Hoarding Riches

A dragon curls up on a pile of treasure inside a cave. The pile is called a hoard. Gold coins, gems, jewelry, and other riches might make up a hoard.

The dragon lays its head down. It is calm. But it watches the area around it carefully. It does not want a human, animal, or another dragon to take its hoard.

Hoarding treasure is just one behavior that people believe is common in dragons. A person's or animal's behavior is the way they act and react. It includes routines such as moving from place to place or eating certain foods. It can also include how a creature interacts with people or animals. Using special

Dragons are symbols of greed in some cultures. This may be why they hoard treasure.

abilities, such as breathing fire, in response to something is a behavior too.

Dragons are not real. But they have appeared in many myths and stories since ancient times. These stories show dragons behaving in all sorts of ways. Some are fierce creatures that prefer to be alone. Others are friendly and live in groups. What are some of the many ways dragons might act?

CHAPTER 1
Basic Behaviors

People of cultures around the world have created, shared, and heard stories about dragons. This means that there is a lot of information about how dragons behave. Some specific behaviors, such as whether a dragon breathes fire or is nice to people, often depend on the culture or myth a dragon comes from. But other behaviors are more general. Two of the most basic dragon behaviors are choosing where they live and what they eat.

Different types of dragons live in different climates.

Heading Home

Dragons live in all parts of the world and all kinds of ecosystems. People often call a dragon's home its den or lair. Most dragons choose to live in nature, far away from people. If you can think of a natural, undisturbed place, a dragon might like to live there.

Some dragons prefer to live deep in forests. They make a den among the trees. Others choose to live on mountains. They might live along the side of the mountain or at the top of a sharp peak. They brave the strong winds and cold

Forests can provide shelter and hiding places for dragons.

Some dragons live up high to keep watch over the land.

weather. Many mountain dragons can leap straight into the sky to fly. Dragons could live in many other places too. These include marshes, deep pools of water, unused castles, and more.

SEE YOU IN THE SEA

Most water-dwelling dragons live near water. Others live underwater! They might live in oceans, lakes, or rivers. Some dragons can breathe underwater. Others hold their breath for hours and only surface for fresh air.

This cave may make a perfect home for a dragon.

The most common home for a dragon is a cave. Caves can be in mountains, along beaches, or anywhere with a lot of stone. Some caves are underground. Caves help protect dragons. For dragons that hoard treasure, a cave is useful for storing it. Caves also help protect dragons from bad weather and intruders.

Most dragons are very protective of their dens.

A mosaic in Istanbul, Turkey, that shows a dragon eating a lizard

Time for Dinner

Dragons have varied diets. Many European dragons are carnivores. They only eat meat. They might hunt for land animals such as cows, deer, or wolves. Some dragons even like to eat humans! Once they find an animal, many will eat it on the spot. But fire-breathing dragons might cook their dinner first.

Dragons that live in or near water eat aquatic animals too. Fish and crocodiles from rivers and streams might be prey for these dragons. Large water-dwelling dragons might hunt for sharks and whales in the sea. Many East Asian dragons eat both aquatic animals and birds.

But not all dragons are meat-eaters. Some also eat plants such as leafy greens, vegetables, and fruits. Certain dragons, such as some Norse dragons, are herbivores and only eat plants.

A dragon's size might affect what it eats. Small dragons prefer plants, bugs, and small animals. Big dragons can catch and eat bigger prey such as pigs and moose.

GORGING ON GOLD

Most dragons eat meat or plants. But some feast on treasure. They eat gold, silver, and even gems.

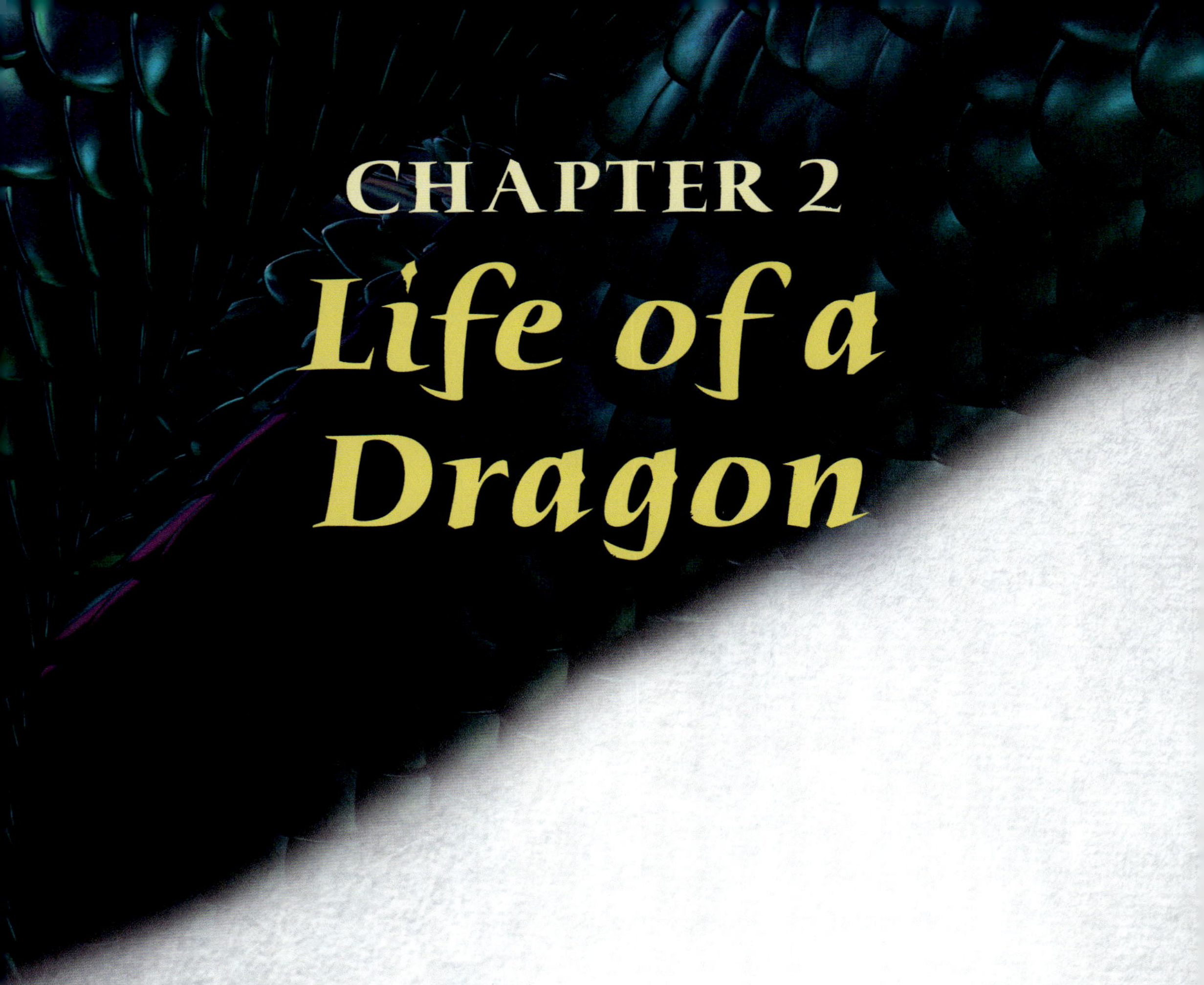

CHAPTER 2
Life of a Dragon

Whether slithering through a river or flying high in the sky, dragons live all over the world. But where they live is just one part of dragon behavior. Another important part is how they live.

Egg to Old Age

A dragon begins as an egg. A female dragon finds a male dragon. They mate and make a nest, often in a cave. The female dragon lays a small group of eggs in the nest. Dragons can lay eggs once a year. But most do not mate that often.

Dragon eggs can come in many shapes and sizes.

Dragons might stay in the egg for two months or more. Then they hatch. Some dragons have an egg-tooth, a sharp bone on their snout that helps them crack the eggshell. Others claw their way out.

HUGE EGGS

Dragon eggs can be huge. In some stories, they are the size of a 50-gallon (189 L) rain barrel.

Not all dragons begin life with their parents, but many do. The parents might teach them how to hunt, eat, and use special abilities such as flight. A dragon might remain with its parents for just a year or two. Or it might stay for more than ten or fifteen years.

Some young dragons grow up on their own.

Dragon hatchlings are usually the same color as their parents.

Dragons have long lifespans. Most are thought to live for hundreds or even thousands of years. Female and male dragons can begin to mate as young adults, between the ages of fifty and one hundred.

Living in groups may help dragons keep control over a larger area.

On Their Own

In some stories, especially modern ones, dragons live in groups or tribes. They might live with several other dragons. Some even live alongside people. But in most myths, dragons live alone. After leaving their parents, they find their own den or lair.

Many dragons are believed to control the area they live in. They pay close attention to who or what comes and goes. When humans, animals, or other dragons enter that area, the dragon that lives there might see them as a threat. It might become stressed or angry. It might even attack or eat the intruder.

FACT VS. FICTION

Dragons usually prefer to be alone.

FACT!

Some dragons live in groups or get along with people. But most would prefer to live alone. Dragons are a type of reptile. Like dragons, most reptiles live alone and only come together to mate. Living alone means they are less stressed and do not have to compete for food.

Some dragons live in ruins of old buildings.

CHAPTER 3
Special Skills

Dragons can live for hundreds of years. They have to spend time eating and sleeping, just like other animals. But many dragons have special hobbies and abilities too.

Making a Hoard

Many dragons hoard treasure. This is especially true for dragons that come from European myths. Their treasure can include special metals such as gold and silver. They might hoard gemstones such as rubies and diamonds. Powerful weapons and magical items may also be of interest to dragons.

Dragons also hoard another special item: knowledge. Many dragons are known for being very wise. They know a lot about the world, and they want to know more. Dragons might gather knowledge about history. They might learn about animals and nature. Some even collect human knowledge such as how to make items and weapons out of metal.

Knowledge-hungry dragons might take over libraries and spend a lot of time learning.

Some dragons use their knowledge to help people. They are so wise that they can offer advice to people facing a tough challenge.

FORTUNE TELLERS

Some dragons, such as the Chinese long, are believed to be able to predict the future.

Chinese long are often seen as good luck.

Some dragons, such as wyverns, use their wings to fly and help them walk.

Skilled with the Elements

Most dragons have special abilities that help them travel, provide for people in need, and more. These abilities are often related to one of the four elements: air, earth, fire, and water. One common ability is flying. Dragons with wings can propel themselves through the air. Many wingless dragons fly too. They might have special organs inside their bodies that help them fly or be so lightweight that they can float. Or they might use magic.

Many dragons have a special connection to nature.

Some dragons have earth powers. They can lift and move around soil and heavy rocks. Others can control plants or make new sprouts spring up from the ground.

Many dragons from European myths can breathe fire. These dragons are often seen as dangerous. They might fly around and breathe fire at people who bother them or who try to take their hoard.

But not all dragons are fire-breathers. Some dragons are skilled with water. The Rainbow Serpent from Aboriginal

Fire breath can be used as an attack or a defense.

An Aboriginal Australian bark painting of a Rainbow Serpent

Australian myths is a snakelike dragon. It is said to bring rainbows when it travels between waterholes in the sky.

In myths from some East Asian countries, such as China and Japan, dragons are known to use water to help people. They

WATCH OUT FOR POISON

Many dragons can control or create water. But some use a different liquid: poison! They might poison something by biting it.

bring rain that helps crops grow. They protect people who are out at sea. Others can control wind. People often believe these East Asian dragons are lucky.

Dragons of All Kinds

Dragons behave in all kinds of ways. Some are friendly. Others are fierce. Some spend their free time flying high in the sky. Others prefer to snake through cool rivers and lakes. What else do you think dragons enjoy doing? What other places might they live, or what other foods might they eat?

Dragons come from cultures and myths throughout the whole world. The way they act in ancient myths might be different from how they act in modern stories. But parts of their behavior might be the same too. People have told all kinds of stories about how dragons act. Now it's your turn! Talk about it with a friend. Maybe you will come up with a different list of dragon behaviors.

A Look at Firedrakes

Some firedrakes live in hot places, such as near a volcano.

Firedrakes get their name from their ability to breathe fire. They are most common in German and Celtic myths but appear in modern stories too. Most drakes have four legs and no wings. But firedrakes often do have wings. Firedrakes hoard treasure. They might breathe fire to protect themselves from an intruder. Or they might do it to stop an intruder from trying to steal their hoard.

Glossary

ability: natural or learned skill

ancient: very old or relating to a time early in history

ecosystem: an area where plants, animals, and everything around them live and work together

element: a force of nature such as air or water

hoard: a supply or fund stored up and often hidden away, or to store and hide something

lifespan: the average number of years a species lives

mate: to produce offspring, or babies

myth: a story often with imaginative creatures, people, and events that explain history, beliefs, or something else

prey: an animal hunted or killed by another animal for food

reptile: a cold-blooded animal that lays eggs and is often covered with scales or other hard body parts

Learn More

Britannica Kids: Dragon
https://kids.britannica.com/kids/article/dragon/353064

Gauthier, Kelly. *The Ultimate Dragon Field Guide: The Fantastical Explorer's Handbook*. Nashville: Applesauce, 2023.

Kaiser, Brianna. *The Science of Dragons: A Field Guide*. Minneapolis: Lerner Publications, 2026.

Kiddle: Dragon Facts for Kids
https://kids.kiddle.co/Dragon

KidsKonnect: Dragon Facts and Worksheets
https://kidskonnect.com/animals/dragon/

Rea, Amy C. *Dragons of Norse Mythology*. Minneapolis: Kids Core, 2024.

Index

Photo Acknowledgments

Image credits: JNBM/Getty Images, p. 5; Warpaintcobra/Getty Images, p. 7; Sylphe_7/Getty Images, p. 8; IanGoodPhotography/Getty Images, p. 9; OhTheHuemanity/Shutterstock, p. 10; FairytaleDesign/Getty Images, pp. 11, 25; James Talalay/Alamy Stock Photo, p. 12; TonisPan/Getty Images, p. 13; eddystocker/Shutterstock, p. 15; Vac1/Shutterstock, p. 16; Crudelitas/Shutterstock, p. 17; MediaProduction/Getty Images, p. 18; Daemon Barzai/Getty Images, p. 19; Shutterstock AI Generator, p. 21; iWUTJRW/Shutterstock, p. 22; dottedhippo/Getty Images, p. 23; Warm_ Tail/Shutterstock, p. 24; Raimund Franken/ullstein bild/Getty Images, p. 26; MasPix/Alamy Stock Photo, p. 28. Design elements: NikonLamp/ Shutterstock; Lukasz Szwaj/Shutterstock; vi73/Shutterstock; T Studio/ Shutterstock; VartB/Shutterstock.

Cover image: Arthur Balitskii/Shutterstock.